Take Off The Mask & Live

JANICE STRICKLIN

Cover Design by Dresbach Studios
Back Cover Author Photo by Eric Dejuan Photography

Library of Congress Control Number: 2019916118

Trade Paperback ISBN: 978-1-7341020-0-0
eBook ISBN: 978-7341020-1-7

Lulu Publishing Services rev. date: 01/03/2020

Pockets of Truth, Inc.
PO Box 380485
Birmingham, AL 35238
Pocketsoftruth@gmail.com

Special Thanks

To the many men and women who— through love, prayer, and encouragement — have helped make this book a reality and for the continual leadership of
The Holy Spirit

Dedication

In memory of my loving daughter Nancy (known as "Nan Lin") whose life taught me these words:

"Life is but a moment; make it an amazing one"

CONTENTS

INTRODUCTION

In a world where deception has become acceptable — even the norm

— We, the body of Christ, find ourselves with a serious identity crisis.

We who are called by His name have been subtly led into a place of personal hiding. For many, this place was not one created by choice, but by the doctrines and traditions of the church world, many of which have nothing to do with God or His Word.

For years, we have been saying, "It is not about religion; it is about relationship." Stop and take a good look around you in the church today.

What has happened to that relationship? It appears we have been slowly moving from relationship to the wearing of "the mask." That mask is covering something, and behind that something is the "real you."

You may not think you have on a mask, or perhaps you had one on at some point but thought you removed it and moved on.

My question is: Are you sure?

By the time you walk through this book your answer to that question may shock you.

Perhaps you are an attorney, renowned physician, business owner, pastor, waitress, school teacher, or church leader with the credentials to prove it. I want you to consider this question: Is that your true identity? Or is that just the work you do and where you find yourself in life? Who are you really?

This book is designed to move you from where you are to who you are.

You are about to see the simple, yet powerful truth of God's Word in new light — a light that will move you from just seeing written Scriptures on a page to empowering you to use them directly in your day-to-day life.

If, while going through the reasons for wearing a mask, we hit something you are dealing with, don't panic; God is not mad at you. As a matter of fact, this book is an expression of His love for you. He knows when "it" showed up in your life. ("It" is anything that stops you from living completely as the original you, a true child of God with all the power, authority, and resources of God being accessed in your life.)

He and I worked together to write this book as a means of escape from the temptation of "it." First Corinthians 10:13 (the Message Bible) says: "No test or temptation that comes your way is beyond the course of what others have had to face. All you need to remember is that God will never let you down; he'll never let you be pushed past your limit; he'll always be there to help you come through it."

The Holy Spirit is here right now to help you through this. He will keep this between you and God.

So embark with me upon this journey of revelation. "For there is nothing covered that shall not be revealed, nor hid that shall not be known" (Luke 12:2).

This revelation will come through the opening of several doors of truth. John 8:32 says: "You shall know the truth and the truth shall make you free." True freedom is God's desire for you.

Ephesians 6:11-17 talks about putting on the whole armor of God with all the different parts of the armor. One part says: "having your loins girt about with truth." The "girt about with truth" refers to a belt used in ancient times, a belt that held things that were necessary to the individuals' life. In this book, as a part of your armor, we are going to use that belt to carry tools for life. **At the end of chapters (1) thru (4), we are going to add a new strategic tool for life to your belt.**

Before we begin this journey together, allow me to make a decree[1] over you. For Job 22:28 says we can decree a thing, and it shall be established.

Therefore, in the name of Jesus Christ, "I decree that as you read this book, you will stand in a place to receive wisdom, counsel, knowledge, a new reverential fear of God, understanding, and prophetic insight. With the skill of a master surgeon, may layers be removed with great accuracy, and may the operation reveal and deal with the roots of the deception causing the mask to emerge. And may "it" be finally completely removed so that your full life, the one your loving father God purposed for you, will spring forth."

So be it.

---

[1] Psalm 2:7 I will declare (announce officially, to state clearly) the decree (order, by law or judicial decision, to fore ordain).

CHAPTER ONE

LET THE JOURNEY BEGIN!!

T he children of God have entered a critical hour where God is now requiring all of us, not just some of us, to be our real selves, the ones He created us to be.

Many of us, in hot pursuit of being the one God created us to be, have done so by going from conference to conference and church service to church service, hearing a good word. Sometimes we get a trickle of change here and there, but still no real lasting change in our lives. As 2 Timothy 3:7 says: "Ever learning and never able to come to the knowledge of the truth."

Truth is the vehicle for real change. There is no real change unless your mind is changed, and your mind will not be changed unless you hear and fully understand. So often we cannot do that because "it" is blocking us. And that thing covering "it" is "the mask."

The first door of truth we are going to open is the truth about the mask. What exactly is this thing called "the mask"?

The Anatomy of the Mask: *"Your secret hiding place"*

There are three types of masks:

- The type that covers just your eyes
- The type that covers your eyes and your nose
- The type that covers your entire face

Keep the following thought in mind as we walk through this explanation:

A mask is either something you created or something that was created for you, but either way, *you are the only one who can remove it.*

Each type of mask affects a different part of your life:

1. **The first mask**, which covers your eyes only, affects your peripheral vision, the part that allows you to see the outer edges to complete the big picture. **This kind of mask leads to tunnel vision.** While you can still see the central details, you can miss the full scope of things. In spiritual terms, this mask would allow you only to see your church, your group, or crew and miss interacting with or even considering the body of Christ at large. It can cause you to miss seeing how what you do and how you do a thing actually fits into the "Kingdom of God". The danger of this is that, what may have started out as a God idea could eventually become just a good idea with no real relevance to God's plan for the Kingdom of God. An example of this could be: Perhaps, God told you He wanted you to start a Bible study group in your home. But later He said He wanted you to expand it to a larger building, including more people. He wants to take your side of town for the Kingdom, but you and your small group connect so well and seem to be doing so much good where you are. Plus you don't want the hassle of a larger responsibility, so you decide what you have is good enough. At that moment, you stopped seeing kingdom and now only see your group. Maybe in your ministry you started out praying about everything, asking God what to do and how to do it. Then your ministry starts to grow very large and you started moving away from asking God what He wants to asking

people what they think you should do, assuming it is what God wants.

2. **The second mask** not only covers your eyes, but it also covers your nose, impacting your ability to distinguish between a bad odor and a good odor. On the spiritual side, **this type of mask would affect your ability to clearly discern.** It can make it difficult to distinguish between the unction of the Holy Spirit and just a feeling. The world is lead by feelings, but sons of God are lead by the Holy Spirit: "For as many as are led by the Spirit of God they are the Sons of God" (Romans 8:14).

3. **The third mask** not only covers your eyes and nose, it also covers one of the most **God-like** features we have, and that's our mouth.

From the mouth, we speak a thing with authority to establish it. We call into existence things that do not already exist. We cast out demons, and we accomplish things on the earth like our Father. For He said: "So is my word that goes out from my mouth: it will not return to me empty, but will accomplish what I desire, and achieve the purpose for which I sent it" (Isaiah 55:11).

The mask can also distort how you see God. Did you notice that each mask includes covering the eyes? When your perspective of God is off, it affects the image you are being transformed into. (If you want proof, just look at the body of Christ today!)

Not only does it affect your view *of* God, but it also affects your vision *from* God. Perhaps your vision started out crystal clear, but as the years went on and it expanded and changed, it may have become a little blurry, or even gone totally off course and given the enemy access in that area.

Now that you see each mask and how it can affect you spiritually,

I want to introduce you to how the mask might function in the everyday life of an individual, perhaps even you.

Functions of the Mask

Some masks are used just for hiding. Since it covers all or part of your face, many people wear it to conceal their true identity. Instead of letting people see their real face, they symbolically are a likeness of a face much like plaster molded to the shape of the face — so it is like your face, but not actually it. *An example of this would be* someone who is hurting emotionally and is crying when they are alone, but when they are around other people they always have a big smile, or they have low self-esteem, but appear confident and self assured when in the presence of others. A person could even be resentful, jealous and angry in their thoughts and emotions inside but, appear to be kind loving and happy on the outside.

A key place this mask could be lurking is on Facebook where individuals can appear to look and be anybody they create and a place where fantasy can be played out anonymously.

Some masks are used for hurting others. This would be a mask of betrayal, which can be used to break trust, mislead, or deceive. The key motive here is to purposefully misrepresent oneself with the intention of hurting someone. *An example of this might be* someone who is very polite to your face, but spreads untrue rumors or gossip about you behind your back. The mask could also be a form of Social Media, where misrepresentation can be used to lure innocent individuals into a place of harm.

Some masks are used for protection. These types of masks consist of a wire or gauze that protects the face from things that would hurt you (think about a catcher's mask in baseball or a mask worn in fencing). The person's face can be seen, but the main job of the mask is protection from external things. *An example of this would be* someone who has vowed to never let anyone get close to them again. Other examples of this could be a hurtful situation between a church member and a pastor or church leader that was not resolved. The wound was not healed, but the member moved on to another ministry with that mask of protection in place to make sure they don't get hurt like that again.

As we further explore the anatomy of the mask, it is crucial to fully understand this next area. It could be the answer to your questions, such as "God, what is going on with me?" "Why is this happening in my life?" "What is standing in my way?" "God, I am standing and believing, but nothing seems to be changing."

The Power of the Mask

The mask has the ability to blind the wearer to the things God has for them. It could muffle your voice and bring disappointment and frustration. It could cause the wearer to bypass the real issues in their life and destroy true vision bringing ruin and often bitterness.

The bottom line is a mask can give the enemy access to your life. It is definitely something to look at if you are wondering why the devil at times has a field day with you.

Everything we have discussed about the mask has been to help you see how serious this thing can be in our lives and how it can affect the "real you."

At this point, perhaps you are seeing how the mask can affect a person and their relationships in terrible ways, but wonder what it has to do with you.

That brings us to the correlation between "it" and "the mask" in the following chapters.

Add to your belt:

Tool 1: If the devil seems to be having a field day in your life, check for access points (places where Satan could have gained legal entity into your life). Use Ephesians 4:22-32 for a list of possible access points. When points of entry are determined then use your authority and power to kick the enemy out and close the door. Luke 10:19, Matthew 18:18-19.

CHAPTER TWO

"IT" AND "THE MASK"

The Mirror

Imagine you walk into a room that contains only one object, an oval mirror in a golden leaf-carved frame. This mirror is just large enough for you to see yourself from the shoulders up. It is not just any mirror; it is unique because it has the ability to allow you to see yourself as you are being transformed into the image of God.

Second Corinthians 3:18 describes us as standing before a mirror that reflects what we should eventually look like as a son or daughter of God and how we are to be representing God on the earth. This transformation process will help you understand how "it" and "the mask" could show up in your life.

Allow me to illustrate.

First you decide to make Jesus the Lord and Savior of your life; so, by faith you tell God you are sorry for your sins, and that you are ready to turn and go another way. You ask Him to forgive you, and you receive Jesus Christ into your heart in an experience the Scripture calls being **born again** (John 3:1-7).

Now you are eager to be like Jesus, so you go to the mirror. The mirror represents the Bible. When you first look into the mirror, you find you don't quite look like Him yet, so you start attending church services where your pastor is teaching the Word of God, you begin to study the Bible, and you receive the Holy Spirit into your life. Each day you go back to the mirror and see that you look a little more like Jesus.

On the first day you went back to the mirror, you noticed your mouth looked like his because you have begun to speak His Word in love. Then on another day, you notice your eyes are starting to look like His because now you are beginning to see people like He sees them through the eyes of love instead of judgment or criticism.

When your focus becomes eternal, it means you are filtering what you see, hear, and think through the Word of God.

On a later trip to the mirror, you notice you have your Father's ears because you have begun to hear Him clearly and be led by His Spirit on a regular basis. Then one day you go to the mirror and you realize you are starting to look a lot like His twin. WOW!!! But then "it" happens.

Now be mindful that "it" can come from anywhere and through anybody. "It" mostly shows up unexpectedly, right in the midst of what you see as a powerful life in God or right in the midst of God using you in some awesome ways.

"It" is anything that steps between you and His "mirror," which holds up the reflection of who you really are — your rights, power, and authority — and begins to distort that image.

When "it" initially shows up in your life, you may immediately recognize "it" and deal with "it." But sometimes "it" may come in the form of an unexpected offense that you don't readily forgive, or at a point of total exhaustion where you are too tired to resist the devil, or at a place where God is using you so much that you begin to mistake God's using you as a measure of your relationship with Him. You know that place where you feel you are so anointed and so powerful that you must really be close to God? (Smile)

An unresolved "it" can open the door to several more "its,"

and at that point, you could find yourself trying to cover "it" up. Hence, out comes **"the mask."**

This cover up is huge. It is not just that things are being covered up. What's the big deal? you ask. "We're all covering up something", you say. Allow me to give you a glimpse of what "it" and "the mask" are covering up.

Second Corinthians 3:18 not only tells us of the transforming power of the Gospel, it gives us insight into the magnitude of the transformation.

The Living Bible version says: "But we Christians have no veil over our faces; we can be mirrors that brightly reflect the glory of the Lord. And as the Spirit of the Lord works within us, we become more and more like Him."

In this verse, we see that we can stand in a place where there is nothing between us and God. We can see him clearly enough to become a true reflection of Him in our everyday life. What that true reflection of Him looks like is part of what "it" and "the mask" are covering.

They are covering the "glory of the Lord."

The word "glory" in the New Testament Greek is "kabodh" and in the Old Testament Hebrew, "doxa." Both allude to the full weight of someone of high importance; in this case, God and His reputation, attributes, character and the full expression of His nature.

"It" and "the mask" are covering you up; hindering you from being the exact replica of and representation of God in your daily life. They are stopping you from using the full potential of what God has put inside of you. When we talk about being more and more like Him, it means to move from "work to work." This "work to work" is demonstrated in the term "true worshipper," (John 4:23) meaning one who worships God with his life by walking out all the work God has put in him — all the gifts, authority, corporations, and works of art, etc.

In essence, this Scripture is saying that at some point, I should be getting a glimpse of God when I see you.

This brings us to another door of truth.

Add to your belt:

Tool 2:

- The world should be seeing transformation in you so much that people start mistaking you for Jesus. They should be saying you are just like your Daddy God.
- When was the last time a stranger recognized you were a Christian without you telling them?
- Does the world notice something different about you? Or do you just blend in?

CHAPTER THREE

THE ORIGINAL YOU

New DNA

I t excites me to even think about His door of truth because behind it is a truth so powerful that it can transform your entire life.

This is the truth about the "original you" — who and what God originally created you to be. This truth begins in Genesis 1 and goes through 2:24. I recommend that you read this in the Amplified version. In these verses, God introduces us to what He did in creating us. This is important to know because something happened between the original you and the real you today. The "original you" and all that you are was lost (separated from God). It talks about this loss in Genesis 3 (NIV). Then we find in John 3:16 and 2 Corinthians 5:18-19, the restoration of, and the full access to, the "original you." The "original you" is how God sees you now. In order to fully embrace the real you, and the freedom that brings, we need to know what you originally had so we can know what has been restored.

We see Jesus Christ coming on the scene, as an expression of God's tremendous love for us after Adam and Eve disobeyed and gave everything over to the enemy of God, Satan. After they disobeyed God, there was a penalty to be paid and that penalty was death. God wanted so badly to be back in relationship with us the way we were, that He was willing to allow His only son to suffer death on behalf of us all (1 Corinthians 15:22). So, we accept what He did through His son Jesus (John 19:1-30) by receiving Him into our heart and lives as our Lord and Savior. By faith through grace, we can walk out this "born again" experience (John 3:1-7).

This "born again" experience immediately gives us access to a wonderful gift that Jesus left for us in the person of the Holy Spirit (John 14:16,17,26). When the Holy Spirit comes into our spirit he brings with him the power we need to walk out this new life in Jesus (Acts 1:8). However, he is not an automatic tenant; **you have to ask him in.** Even though he was present when you were born again, he wants to have full access to you so he can lead and guide you into all truth. It is as simple as asking God to fill you with His Spirit. This is important because Romans 8:9 says: "You, however, are not in the realm of the flesh but are in the realm of the Spirit, if indeed the Spirit of God lives in you. And if anyone does not have the Spirit of Christ, they do not belong to Christ."

So right here, I want you to pause and answer these questions: Are you sure that the Spirit of God lives in you? If so, what makes you sure?

If your answer is no, then take a moment and ask God to fill you with His Spirit. And He will. Restored and empowered. Now you are ready for your next door of truth.

New DNA

This door of Truth is so wonderful because at the moment you were "born again", God became your father, and it is His DNA that you received.

This is done in the same way as medical science says your DNA or your genetic make-up comes from your parents.

Think about this: We have been told in many church settings that God has a plan for our lives and a purpose for our being here. The question is what is it? Well, locked in your new DNA is the answer to your true identity and your purpose for being.

Back in Genesis 1, God's DNA is explained. God began by saying we are created in His image and His likeness. He describes you as having dominion and authority and that your purpose is to be fruitful, multiply, replenish and subdue the earth.

- **Dominion** means to have the power or unchallenged authority over something.
- **Replenish** means to make full or complete again by supplying what is lacking.
- **Subdue** means to conquer and bring into subjection.

So, the "real you" — whether you are a male or a female — as a child of God has been given power to prosper, reproduce and make disciples to increase God's kingdom. You're also to supply the earth with whatever it needs and to bring it under His control by superior force. You are given the power and right to govern and control it, to have sovereign (ultimate, indisputable) authority over all the earth and everything in the sea and on land.

It is true when Jesus came and died for us, He restored the ability for mankind to have the same power and authority over the earth as God intended in Genesis. Jesus took back what Adam had given away.

We were born into a sin-driven world and taught from birth how to live and obey the laws and principles of Satan's world system. Through Jesus, we now have been moved out of the kingdom of darkness into the kingdom of God's dear son (Colossians 1:13). If you are a follower of Christ, you have a new citizenship and renewed reason for being on the earth. **You are here to reestablish your Fathers' kingdom on earth by regaining His territory and recruiting more into His kingdom to take back territory until His rule through us again is sovereign on the earth.**

This is what we are actually supposed to be doing. Think about it: Just like Jesus had the ability to speak to the tree and it died, you were given back that same authority. "As He (Christ) is so are we in this world" (I John 4:17).

Along with that authority comes everything you will ever need to live out your life as a true son or daughter of God. (Reference 2 Peter 1:2-4 to see the magnitude of this.)

Thus, the "real you" is what "it" and "the mask" are ultimately covering.

So far, we have been talking about how wonderful the "real you" is and your benefits. But let's dig a little deeper and look at some consequences that come into place when you are not living as the "real you."

I want you to take another look at the phrase "work to work," the doing part of you being like your Daddy God.

James 1:23-24 states the following: "For if anyone is a hearer of the word and not a doer, he is like a man observing his natural face in a mirror; for he observes himself, goes away and immediately forgets what kind of man he was"(NKJ). "Don't fool yourself into thinking that you are a listener when you are anything but, letting the Word go in one ear and out the other. Act on what you hear! Those who hear and don't act are like those who glance in the mirror, walk away, and two minutes later have no idea who they are, or what they look like" (MSG).

Being a doer is extremely important. For some reason we think we can pick and choose what we do or don't do. You really are not your own, you really have been purchased with a price. (1 Corinthians 6:19, 20).

You need to understand that your doing is tied to your eternity. What we do and how we live here on earth will not determine where we spend eternity, but it will determine what rewards we will receive in eternity.

Because we are saved by faith through grace, we will be going to Heaven, but what will your lifestyle be when you get there?

Will you rule or will you serve(Matthew 25:21-23)? Will there be rewards or is your account empty (1Corinthians 3:13-15)? I have inserted Scripture references above because I want you to be able to go back and read them in their entirety to get the full picture of the connection between doing and eternity.

Second Corinthians 5:10 says: " For we must all appear before the judgment seat of Christ; that every one may receive the things done in his body, according to that he hath done, whether it be good or bad." This Scripture implies you have done something, and not only have you done something, but you have done something in God's kingdom.

Stop here for a moment and think about this question:

What are you doing for the kingdom of God?

Notice, I did not ask what are you doing in your local church? Perhaps what you are doing in your local church is not affecting the kingdom at all. Not only will we be held accountable for what we did, but also for what we did not do, but should have done.

Now even in the midst of all this power and knowledge of the "real you" the world is still waiting to see God in us on a consistent basis. So why is that?

Let's take a look at one possibility: Maybe it is because there has been little or no true lasting change taking place in the lives of the body of Christ. As we mentioned earlier, it is not because we have not been hearing His Word; true change has not happened because the Word heard has not been truly comprehended.

Therefore, there has been little increase in faith, bringing little to no open evidence of who God is on the earth within our daily lives because out of comprehension or understanding comes revelation, and out of revelation comes faith, and out of faith comes the evidence of who God is.

Allow me to show you just how powerful this comprehension

is. Now keep in mind we are taking about truth because I am about to mess with what I call a "sacred cow" in the church.

Have you heard the statement "God is the God of the breakthrough"?

Have you heard pastors say your breakthrough is coming or you are about to breakthrough? Are you are waiting on your breakthrough? If your answer is yes, then my question is WHY?

A breakthrough insinuates that you are on one side of a wall and you are trying to go through the wall to get what is on the other side of it. Well I have news for you. There really is no wall between you and what you want, so why are you trying to breakthrough to something you already have?

In 2 Peter 1:3, the writer states: "According as his divine power hath (past tense) given unto us all things that pertain unto life and godliness, through the knowledge of him that hath called us to glory and virtue."

In Matthew 16:19, Jesus told Peter that He would give him the keys to the kingdom and that whatsoever he bound on earth would be bound in Heaven and whatsoever he loosed on earth shall be loosed in Heaven.

God and Jesus have already done all they are going to do — it is now up to us. God is trying to get us to do more than just talk about the keys to the kingdom; He wants us to use them. You don't have to tear down a door that you have the keys to. Those keys represent that power and authority that has been restored to us. The real issue is whether you know how to put the keys in the door and turn the lock or whether you even know where your keys are.

Second Corinthians 1:20 states: "For all the promises of God in him are yea, and in him Amen, unto the glory of God by us." This means all those promises God made to us are already happening through Christ Jesus.

So, the answer to "Father, can I have...?" is already a yes. "Father I need…" "Here it is."

In talking about comprehending God's Word, God wants us to be like a little child. For example, a little boy asks his mom: "Mommy, can I have some ice cream when we get home?" She says yes. At that point, the child knows in his head and in his heart, that when he gets home, he is going to get ice cream. As a matter of fact, he is so confident that he starts telling his sister: "When I get home, I am going to get some ice cream." By now, he's already thinking about what flavor to choose and whether he wants it on a cone or not; As soon as the car pulls up to the house, he dashes into the kitchen and stands there patiently waiting for Mom to come in so he can start eating his ice cream.

Now that's faith.

Some of what has happened to the body of Christ is that it has gotten caught up in the steps and formulas of substituting works for faith. You know the ones we read in a book on answered prayer: "Seven steps to answered prayer" or "Five steps to your healing" or "Twelve steps to a successful marriage." Now, understand I am not against any resources that God has put in your life. Just make sure that all your focus is not caught up in the steps rather than caught up in God. For instance, in successful marriage books they may suggest you plan a date night each week and a family Bible study each week, etc. You could get so caught up in trying to make those things happen that you unknowingly move your confidence for a good outcome to the steps and away from God. Then comes the comment: "I followed all the steps, so God, why didn't it work?"

Faith will cause you to do something, but just because you are doing something, does not mean it is faith. When we substitute our stuff for His Word we make the Word powerless in our lives.

It is easy, but we have complicated it.

The Word tells us that without faith, it is impossible — not just hard — to please God. Here we need to apply the KISS (Keep It Simple Saints) principle:

1. What is faith?
   Answer: Believing you have something you can't see (with the natural eye).
2. Have faith in what?
   Answer: The finished work of Jesus Christ (God's truth that you are connected back to God as a son with all the benefits — the "original you").
3. How do we get faith?
   Answer: By hearing and hearing (comprehending) the Word of God.

Faith gets you the tangible, physical results.

So, how much Word are you hearing? Let me help you put this into perspective:

- What is your TV to the Word ratio?
- Your work to the Word ratio?
- Your shopping to the Word ratio?
- Your iPhone or Instagram to the Word ratio?
- Your Facebook or Twitter to the Word ratio?

In Joshua 1:8, God said to Joshua: "This book of the law shall not depart out of thy mouth; but thou shall meditate therein day and night, that thou may observe to do according to all that is written therein: for then thou shall *make thy way prosperous, and then thou shall have good success.*"

So when you put the Word in your heart and begin to do it, the things you do, will cause you to do well, and become successful in each area that you apply it to.

For instance, when you apply the Scripture that says: "Be slow to speak, swift to hear, slow to anger," you could find your stress levels diminishing and anxiety and frustration becoming less dominate in your life.

By now you are probably saying "Okay I get it, I need more of God's Word, but I shouldn't have to have the whole Bible studied before I start to live the way God created me to live". What if I am not experiencing the power and authority that was restored to me as a child of God? What's the hold up; what is stopping me from walking in this?

Remember when we were in the room with the mirror and "it" showed up and was not dealt with and "it" became covered with a mask?

If you have an "it" in your life, then that is what's stopping you.

Add to your belt:

Tool 3:

- If you ever start to forget how powerful you are as a child of God, just remember these words: "My daddy is God."
- When Satan starts to get on your nerves, remind him that the "real you" is not just a mere man or woman, you are both human and divine, and the divine you has been given power over all the power of the enemy and nothing shall by any means hurt you (Luke 10:19).

This brings us to what I call your personal moment of truth.

Are you ready? Take a deep breath and breathe out slowly, then turn the page.

CHAPTER FOUR

IDENTIFYING YOUR "IT"

Hidden and Don't Know It

Consider putting yourself in a quiet comfortable place so you will be able to, without any distractions, ponder this thought:

"Could there possibly be an 'it' hiding in my life?"

Now bring up the thoughts of the powerful and authoritative you that God created. Is that the person you see when you look in the mirror?

You may be asking, "How can you have an "it" and not know it?"

Remember in the introduction of this book, we talked about this thing called deception? Sometimes situations and circumstances — even people — can come into our lives and we, for whatever reason, don't properly deal with them, and they can open us up to deception.

But don't worry the Holy Spirit is right here. He has your hand and He is going to walk you right up to this thing, very slowly and gently with great care to uncover "it." Trust Him.

Let's begin with an explanation and illustration of how deception can develop in your life. Did you know you can do a wrong thing so long that your life begins to conform to it? What was noticeable at first — over time — begins to become your norm. When something is your normal, there is a tendency to forget that it is not what was originally intended.

You can walk away and be gone so long from the mirror (the

truth of the Word), that the Scripture says you forgot what you originally saw in the mirror.

This reminds me of an illustration I saw a female speaker present during a church service once. When she reached the podium on stage, she looked down and had everyone notice that the shoes she was wearing were on the wrong feet. It looked quite awkward. She made it very clear she knew that they were on the wrong feet. She explained they were that way because she was doing a test. Then she started to walk back and forth across the stage and began another part of her message. She talked about how we can let the wrong thing go on so long that we forget it is going on, and how— at some point — it begins to look right. Sure enough, by the time she was half way into the message that is exactly what happened. As she progressed in the message, the shoes on the wrong feet became less and less noticeable; so much so that by the end of her message, if you weren't constantly looking at her shoes, you would think that her shoes were on the correct feet.

It is amazing how we can walk in a wrong thing so long that we start to accept it and adapt to it. At first, it is uncomfortable (like the shoes) and it may even hurt, but then we start to conform to this thing until it begins to feel right.

So just maybe there is an "it" in your life hiding behind a mask —something hiding the "real you" and you don't know it.

In order to get to the root of this matter, we need to begin by looking at some **reasons for wearing a mask.** Within these reasons, perhaps we can begin to identify what "it" is being covered up and why there may be a reason for the mask in the first place.

1. Some wear a mask as a form of identify.

Perhaps, what is hidden is the fact that you really don't know your calling. Are you a missionary, an apostle, a prophet, evangelist, pastor, teacher, or are you in search mode for what God has gifted you with and called you to do? Ephesians 4:1-16 tells us that God setup different spiritual gifts to be used in the body of Christ to help all of us grow up in Him. These spiritual gifts are often expressed as ministry work within the confines of the local church.

Sometimes we may display some of the characteristics of a gift yet we are not called to operate in the office of that gift but, other people see it and tell us that this is what we are. So, we begin to operate based on what people say. For instance, I may be an evangelist, but my mask displays me as a pastor.

Or perhaps you did not get a clear word from God. Maybe God told you to

teach His people and you thought He meant to start a church. Now, after putting your life into what was a wrong interpretation or an incomplete word, you feel stuck; you are in church ministry because you missed God.

God expects us to come to Him and allow the Holy Spirit to show us which of these areas we are to work in. **As we take the time to know Him** through His Word, He reveals what He wants us to do with our lives.

The hiding often comes when people around us think we know what our calling is and to save face when we are around others, our mask looks like what they think we are and not who God actually called us to be. This kind of falseness keeps the "real you" hidden from others as well as yourself, and keeps you from fulfilling who God has called you to be.

2. Some wear the mask to cover up stuff they have done or are doing.

For instance, this mask may cover up such behavior as sleeping around with someone you're not married to, watching pornography, being involved in homosexuality or lesbianism, harboring bitterness, or holding on to resentment. When we do these things, it opens us up to denial, which can open your life to deception.

The power of denial could begin with a simple statement such as: "Well, I just want to try this one time, I am not going to keep doing this. I just want to see what it feels like." Or it might look like: "I will forgive them, but not today." Once the door of deception is open it can become normal, and your new normal can over take your life.

Then, what looks right may not be right, and what looks good may not be from God. These things can bring about shame, fear, and hurt that we don't want others to see. And then comes the hiding.

3. Some wear the mask to cover things that were done or are being done to them.

This can include such things as wife beating, verbal abuse, molestation and spousal rape. Often times the hurt never fully heals. When these things are not addressed, but merely covered by a mask that smiles and says "I am blessed and highly favored," then the Holy Spirit is not given the opportunity to bring wholeness.

God has positioned people in the body of Christ who He has equipped to help that person with the love and confidentiality necessary for their healing, but they must first be willing to come out of hiding and ask for help. They don't have to fear because when they ask the Holy Spirit, He will lead them to the right doors for help, and also lead others to them.

4. Some wear a mask because they are like Moses.

Once Moses had the glory of God on him (which represents the presence of God), but he covered his face when it departed. Perhaps at one time the presence of God was very evident in your life. You were excited about and moving in the things the Holy Spirit was instructing you to do through God's Word. You talked to God all the time. You were what some Christians call being "on fire for God." But at some point, your fire went from super hot to just hot and then to a constant medium hot. Now it is a good constant, but common, flame that appears to fit right in with the majority of the body of Christ.

This could happen in a number of ways, but some key ways are: Getting too busy to spend time with God and deciding you know what He wants instead of asking Him. Are you trying to hide that you no longer walk in that place with God?

Unfortunately, some of you may feel like you were forced to put on a mask. Some of you may have put on little pieces of the mask at a time over the years. For some, it was based on a subtle move of the enemy or getting caught up in the excitement of the moment and stepping over into the wrong place, but being too ashamed to step back.

But whatever your reason for the mask, be assured you have the power dwelling in you to remove the mask and whatever it's covering.

As we walk through chapter five (and quite a bit of scripture),we will deal with possible oppositions to removing the mask.

Just as John 8:32 says: You shall know the truth and the truth shall make you free." and John 17:17 says: "Sanctify them through **thy truth: thy word is truth**," we want to use truth as a tool to help expose the things that may be holding the "real you" hostage.

Because truth is so powerful, as you are coming into the

knowledge of the truth about what has been hidden in your life, you will begin to experience some freedom and be made aware that God already knows. He is not waiting to find out about you. He was there at the beginning and is here now, so take heart and move forward.

New life awaits you.

Now that we have gone through the possibilities of "the mask" and whatever "it" is that might be covered up, I recommend you take a moment to pause and take a serious and honest look at where you are in your life and your relationship with God.

Ask yourself again: Are there any "its" in my life? If so, am I covering them up with a "mask"?

Take your time; there can be great power in the pause. There comes a time in each of our lives when we need to pause, ponder, and take an inward look. We need to allow the Holy Spirit to reveal the parts of us we were too busy to address or are just plan avoiding on purpose. After all, we are the light of the world and our world today is in such great darkness, we cannot afford to have our true light hidden.

Before we start the removal process, allow me to make sure you are fully on board with me.

If you are one of those who still don't think you have a mask on or have an "it" to deal with, I would like for you to answer the following questions. (As you answer, keep in mind "it" is anything that stops you from living completely as the original you, a true child of God with all the power, authority, and resources of God being accessed in your life.)

- Do you really want to live like a child of a God or just live like a good church member?
- Are you willing to be as extreme about your faith as those who are literally willing to die for theirs?

- Do you really comprehend what God is saying in His Word for you to do? Comprehension means understanding to the point of action.
- Is the enemy having a field day in your neighborhood or even in your house?
- Do you really love God? Are you keeping His commandments?
- What "it" is stopping you? Are we ready to deal with "it" now?

You cannot put this off any longer. The Father is ready to bring your good intensions to action.

We live in a time when there is uncovering of the mask going on from the highest offices in the world's system all the way to the church house. Hidden things are being revealed. For example, it used to be that when a politician took an office, it would sometimes be years before his or her dirt came out. But now, even before they take office, confessions or secrets are coming out.

Even some church leaders are being exposed in areas of immorality (sexual misconduct) according to Scripture. We have not even started talking about what is going on in the world's system — human trafficking, terrorism, and utter abandonment of God's laws. We may call these the "big sins" but sin is simply disobedience to God, which comes in many forms.

Even these are not the major problem in the kingdom of God.

The problem is with what we call every day Christians — us. Christians are being exposed as "unbelieving believers" as they question where God is and what He's doing.

All of this may seem like too much, but God has sent you.

In the next two chapters, we will deal with the components of removing "it" and thus, "the mask," and freeing you to finally live your new life.

Add to your belt:

Tool 4:

- Remember that no matter where you are in life, God is always present in you. So whatever you are dealing with today, right this moment, God says: "I am with you, I will never leave you, nor will I forsake you" (Hebrews 13:5). No matter what "it" is, nothing is hard for God. Nothing is impossible for Him to handle (Matthew 19:26) (Mark 9:23) (Luke 18:27).

- No matter what trap the enemy seems to have set, your Father God, says: "With every temptation there is a means of escape because no weapon formed against you shall prosper" (1 Corinthians 10:13).

CHAPTER FIVE

HELP!

My Mask is Stuck

If you feel like you can't get rid of the "it" in your life, there may be some addictions or strongholds involved. Otherwise, you would have dealt with "it" by now.

First, let's look at possible issues stopping you from removing "it" and "the mask."

ISSUES:

1. You are not willing or ready to deal with your "it"

Dear friend, what are you waiting for? I encourage you not to wait any longer. You must make the decision today to deal with this. God is holding you accountable. He loves you and wants to free you from "it," but you must repent and turn to Him.

Romans 13:11,12 says: "And that, knowing the time, that now it is high time to awake out of sleep: for now is our salvation nearer than when we believed. The night is far spent, the day is at hand: let us therefore cast off the works of darkness, and let us put on the armor of light."

2. You are rationalizing your behavior with that of someone else's.

You may be thinking you are just as good as someone else, and if they are doing "it" then it must not be that big of a deal. It is not about how much we can sin and get away with. Romans 6:15 says: "What then? Shall we sin, because we are not under the law, but under grace? God forbid." We should be about how much we love God. True love for God is expressed through our obedience to His Word.

3. You are justifying why "it" is okay.

You might be telling yourself "it" is ok because God is still using me in a mighty way. There may even be some pride in it as you tell yourself: "Look at all the people being blessed through my work." But, keep this in mind: what God is doing through you is not a measure of His relationship with you. You must cultivate that on a personal one- on-one basis with Him.

4. You are having trouble trusting God.

We may do all the things we think we should: quote Mark 11: 23, go to church services and conferences and make loud declarations around Scripture, but we sometimes miss an important truth needed for that Scripture to work in our lives. It requires us to live in constant dependence and trust in God. We need to be thoroughly convinced He is faithful, dependable and trustworthy.

You might not trust God for real; not for real for real (as a friend of mine often says). You may claim to know Him, but when did you become *acquainted* with Him? How can you trust someone you don't really know? I don't mean know "about" Him, but know Him well enough to trust Him with every little detail of your life?

Ask yourself: Do I trust Him when I am stripped of certain things? In what pockets or areas of my life do I not fully trust God? Could it be in the area of healing — both physical and emotional— or maybe in the area of finances or time?

You may be very successful by the worlds' standards, and where you once felt you had to trust God in order to make it, now you have arrived and don't feel the need to have to trust Him. If you feel that way, remind yourself of Revelation 3:17; "Because you say, I am rich, and increased with goods, and have need of nothing; and know not that thou art wretched, and miserable, and poor, and blind, and naked:"

To deal with trust issues, you must first identify where you have them. At the base of your trust issues is your belief system. Hebrews 11:6 says: "But without faith it is impossible to please Him, for he who comes to God must believe that He is, and that He is a rewarder of those who diligently seek him." Although we often focus only on the last half of this verse, we must remember our part of the bargain.

My question to you is — do you still believe that He is…? (Put whatever you need behind that "is.") Or have you been disappointed so many times, or become so tired of waiting that perhaps you are wondering if He really is? You will need to re-evaluate where you really are in this part of your relationship with Him. Just know that He has never walked away, and He is there waiting on you.

5. You fear the next steps.

Fear comes from several places. You may be afraid of what people will say, which could be tied to ego and pride issues. Those also could be tied to self-esteem and shame issues, which could be ties to sin issues. At the heart of it, we often don't fully understand how complete His forgiveness and love for us is. A great remedy for fear is 1 John 4:18: "There is no fear in **love**; but **perfect love casts out** fear: because fear hath torment. He that fears is not made **perfect** in **love**." One thing we can always be assured of is that fear does not come from God, because 2 Timothy 1:7 says: "For God hath not given us the **spirit of fear**; but **of** power, and **of** love, and **of** a sound mind."

6. You are dealing with immaturity.

Perhaps you have chosen to stay on milk and have never ventured into your calling on the earth. You're just content being a house-worker. A house-worker is someone who works in a local church as a paid employee or a volunteer. Although those functions are important and necessary for ministry work and growth, these positions can become dangerous if an individual sees his or/her place in the kingdom of God as being only their local church, not the greater kingdom.

As you grow in Christ, you must be open to your specific call within the body of Christ at large. Your calling may be the "ministry of helps" in your congregation, but at some point, God will call for that beyond the walls of your local assembly. If you are not mature enough for your focus to be eternal, then your life will just be about Saint 123 Church or First Blue Church on the corner. God calls you to so much more. There's no reason to be afraid He equips you, as well.

In Galatians 4:1-7 God calls us to so much more. Dwell on these beautiful words "Now I say, that the heir, as long as he is a child, differs nothing from a servant, though he be lord of all; but is under tutors and governors until the time appointed of the father. Even so we, when we were children, were in bondage under the elements of the world: But when the fullness of the time was come, God sent forth His son, made of a woman, made under the law, to redeem them that were under the law, that we might receive the adoption of sons. And because ye are sons, God hath sent forth the Spirit of His son into your hearts, crying, "Abba, Father", "Wherefore thou art no more a servant, but a son; and if a son, then an heir of God through Christ."

We must be more than just house workers if we are going to function as children of God. Immaturity limits power. Satan cannot stop you from being a son but you can allow him to stop you from ruling and reigning.

7. You are not willing to abandon your sin.

When you are wrapped in willful sin, you are choosing to wear the mask to cover your choice to sin. I encourage you to read Romans 14:23 and James 1:13-15 to learn more about this.

In an earlier chapter, we asked the question why was what you had been asking God for being held up? Part of that answer is found in Proverbs 28:13: "He that covers his sins **shall not prosper**: but whoso confesses and forsakes them **shall** have mercy."

I know that it might be difficult to admit that perhaps some of these issues may be in your life, but that is okay because all of us have some things in our lives that we have not yet dealt with. But, God is not angry with us. He just wants you free to experience all that He has planned for you.

So, go ahead, dig deep, address any of these that may have been hiding in your life, and let's get on to the "real you."

CHAPTER SIX

TIME TO REMOVE "THE MASK"

And Deal With "IT"

For those of you who are ready to remove your mask and allow God to deal with "it," I have some instructions for you:

First, you need to take time to reexamine and ponder each of the reasons your mask may be stuck. I have *listed them below.* (There are more details in chapter five.)As you review each one, allow the Holy Spirit to fully reveal to you which ones are affecting your life. Luke 12:2 says: For there is **nothing** covered that shall not be revealed; neither **hid**, that shall not be known."

You must be willing for the Holy Spirit to expose any and everything to you about these issues. You may find some of this to be hard, but let me encourage you with Hebrews 12:11. "For the time being no discipline brings joy, but seems sad *and* painful; yet to those who have been trained by it, afterwards it yields the peaceful fruit of righteousness" (right standing with God and a lifestyle and attitude that seeks conformity to God's will and purpose). You can rejoice knowing that God is doing this "for your good" because He loves you. Now that's great news.

Whatever has you stuck it's time to deal with **"IT":**

Let's Begin (Here's the list)

1. You are not willing or ready to deal with your "it"
2. You are rationalizing your behavior with that of someone else's

3. You are justifying why "it" is okay
4. You are having trouble trusting God
5. You fear the next steps
6. You are dealing with immaturity
7. You are not willing to abandon your sin

This is not by any means an exhaustive list, so the Holy Spirit may show you things not on this list that are specific to you.

The second thing is to come clean with God. I have placed a sample prayer below to get you started, but I encourage you to read it then make it your own and get personal with God.

Prayer:

"Father God, in the name of Jesus,

I am coming to you thanking you for your love, your patience and your mercy toward me. I recognize that I have been covering up things that have stopped me from walking completely as your daughter or son. I have been hiding because (*state your reason*). I call those things sin and I repent of them and I ask you to forgive me.

I am now ready to remove the mask and allow you to deal with whatever is in my life and my heart that has been hindering me from truly seeing and reflecting you. Help me to remove this mask. I don't want to be fake in any area of my life. As an act of my faith I am removing the mask now in the name of Jesus. Amen"

I now suggest that you put your hands to your face as if to remove an imaginary mask, and then cast it aside throwing it to the ground.

Know that your mask will hit the ground and be broken into thousands of pieces, it will be destroyed. **REMOVE THE MASK NOW!!**

Now Let's Deal With "it"

Once the mask is destroyed, the Holy Spirit is now ready to help you work on your "it"(s) so just yield to Him.

I pray Hebrews 12:1-2 over you right now, "… let us lay aside every weight, and the sin which does so easily beset us, and let us run with patience the race that is set before us, looking unto Jesus the author and finisher of our faith…."

Step 1:

Look back at chapter four to help you identify your "it(s)".

At this point, perhaps you may be one of those who will have to make some major decisions to release your past or release some people. Either way you are stepping into a new relationship with Him; one that you have never been in before. Be assured He is with you throughout this transition. He will hear you and help you through each part. (For reference, see 2 Corinthians 1:20, Hebrews 13:5, John 16:23, 1John 5:14, 15, and 1 Peter 5:7).

Remember, God is not angry with you. He just loves you so much He wants you to be free. He has so much in store for you that you haven't been able to access — both tangible and intangible things. He is waiting on you.

Step 2:

Now you need to begin by confessing thing(s) to Him and asking Him for forgiveness. First John 1:9 says: "If we confess our sins, he is **faithful and just to forgive** us our sins, **and to** cleanse us from all unrighteousness."

Confessing merely means to agree with God; that the "it" is a sin. As you repent; you are releasing "it" to Him and turning away from "it", that's your part. The forgiveness and cleansing that follows is His part. Allow me to share a visual of what that looks like.

He once described the cleansing part to me as approaching a chalk board that was covered with scribbling. Someone takes an eraser and removes all the chalk, and then takes a water-soaked towel and removes even the residual of the chalk. At the moment you repent, He doesn't just forgive the present sins you are addressing; He clears off all your sins and places you back in the position you were in before Adam disobeyed. All of your unrighteousness is removed and the slate is completely clean. You then have all rights, privileges, power and authority restored. Most of all, you have full access to Him.

Step 3:

Now be open to the Holy Spirit for the strategy for moving forward. He will lead you step-by-step into this new place. Each "it" is different and requires a unique resolution. Let me give you an example. Perhaps someone hurt you deeply and unforgiviness and even bitterness has kept you from walking in your true sonship.

This may require a face-to-face forgiveness or spending time in a prayer closet releasing them through forgiveness. In the case of willful sin, you will have to stop the sin and maybe even sever a relationship entirely. The Holy Spirit will direct you to the steps that may involve counseling, new training, new friends, or even physical relocation, but they will all involve change that is directed by God.

For some of you, this new you may look drastically different from the old you. The change may be so drastic that others may not recognize you.

It is kind of like what I experienced with a friend when we were teenagers. This friend wore makeup and her skin always looked flawless, but I did not know just how much makeup she wore until we went on an overnight band trip. We were roommates, but I had never seen her without the makeup. The next morning I saw her without it and oh my! If I had seen her on the street at that moment, I would not have known her.

That being said, some people are going to look at you a little strange at first, but don't think anything of it. You are just looking more like Jesus that's all.

This step may take a few days or even a few months, but every day you will experience more and more of your new life. Just know this: "But as it is written, **Eye hath not seen**, nor ear heard, neither have entered into the heart of man, the things which God **hath** prepared for them that love him" (1 Corinthians 2:9).

— I pray that as you daily return to the mirror of the Word, you will see the real you created in the image and likeness of God with all the power, authority and provision of Father GOD!!—

NOW LIVE!!

In this last section of the book I have listed several Scriptures that represent the kind of life God desires for you. A life He planned for you before the foundation of the world. This life of peace, power, protection and provision all for the asking belongs to you. It is an expression of His unconditional love for you.

Jeremiah 29:11 (The Message)
I know what I'm doing. I have it all planned out—plans to take care of you, not abandon you, plans to give you the future you hope for.

Psalms 16:11(KJV)
Thou wilt show me the path of life: in thy presence is fullness of joy; at thy right hand there are pleasures for evermore.

1 Corinthians 2:9 (KJV)
But as it is written, **Eye** hath **not seen**, nor ear heard, neither have entered into the heart of man, the things which God hath prepared for them that love him.

2 Peter 1:2-4 (KJV)
Grace and peace be multiplied unto you through the knowledge of God, and of Jesus our Lord, According as his divine power hath given unto us all things that pertain unto life and godliness, through the knowledge of him that hath called us to glory and virtue: Whereby are given unto us exceeding great and precious promises: that by these ye might be partakers of the divine nature, having escaped the corruption that is in the world through lust.

Luke 12:32(KJV)

Fear not, little flock; for it is your Father's good pleasure to give you the kingdom.

Ephesians 3:20(NIV)

Now to him who is able to do immeasurably more than all we ask or imagine, according to his power that is at work within us...

Matthew 7:7, 8(KJV)

Ask and it shall be given you; seek, and ye shall find; knock, and it shall be opened unto you. For every one that asketh receiveth and he that seeketh findeth; and to him that knocketh it shall be opened.

Ephesians 6:10 (KJV) Finally, my brethren, be strong in the Lord, and in the power of his might.

From This Day Forward May Your Life Never Be the Same

For more information about Pockets of Truth, Inc. (our 501C3 Tax exempt organization) or how to book the author for speaking engagements, please Contact: Janice Stricklin at: pocketsoftruth@gmail.com or visit our Website: www.pocketsoftruth.com

www.ingramcontent.com/pod-product-compliance
Lightning Source LLC
Chambersburg PA
CBHW031615040426
42452CB00006B/531